Keynotes

**Essential piano repertoire
from across the ages**

selected and edited by John Lenehan

Grades 2 – 3 · Early Intermediate – Intermediate

This edition © 2005 by Faber Music
First published in 2005 by Faber Music Ltd
3 Queen Square London WC1N 3AU
Cover by Økvik Design
Music processed by Jackie Leigh
Printed in England by Caligraving Ltd
All rights reserved

ISBN 0-571-52321-8

To buy Faber Music publications or to find out about the full range of titles
available please contact your local music retailer or Faber Music sales enquiries:

Faber Music Ltd, Burnt Mill, Elizabeth Way, Harlow CM20 2HX
Tel: +44 (0)1279 82 89 82   Fax: +44 (0)1279 82 89 83
sales@fabermusic.com   fabermusic.com

FABER *ff* MUSIC

Contents

Teachers' notes and audio samples are available for free from fabermusic.com

Gigue

Imagine you are having a conversation in this piece. Your right hand has plenty to say but as soon as there is an opportunity, the left hand nips in and takes it! All ends happily though, with both in perfect agreement.

Georg Philipp Telemann
(1681–1767)

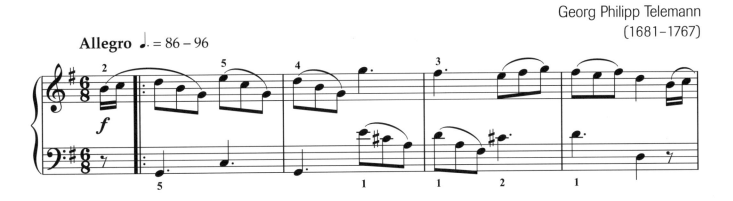

Andante No.37
from The Chelsea Notebook

When Mozart was eight he lived for a time in London. He liked to improvise pieces at the keyboard, and this is typical of his early style – elegant and happy.

Wolfgang Amadeus Mozart
(1756–1791)

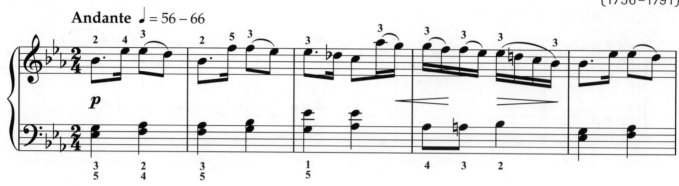

Burglar music

In the early days of cinema (before there was sound), music was played – often on the piano – to create the right mood. This is one of those pieces. Imagine the burglar creeping around and getting a big scare in bar/measure 4.

John Stepan Zamecni
(dates unknow

The wild horseman
from **Album for the Young Op.68**

Schumann wrote his *Album for the Young* as a present for his son's seventh birthday. It included more than 40 pieces like this, written in less than a fortnight! Emphasize the *sforzatos* in both hands, but let your left hand take centre stage when it has the tune.

Robert Schumann
(1810–1856)

In a swing
from Sports and Pastimes

Satie was one of music's greatest eccentrics, and his music often contains humorous nonsense text. Imagine your left hand is swinging back and forth between its two notes. Try to play it with your eyes closed.

Erik Satie
(1866–1925)

Slowly ♩ = 36 or slower

It is my heart that swings and swings.

And never gets dizzy.

As if it has tiny feet!

Will it want to come back to me?

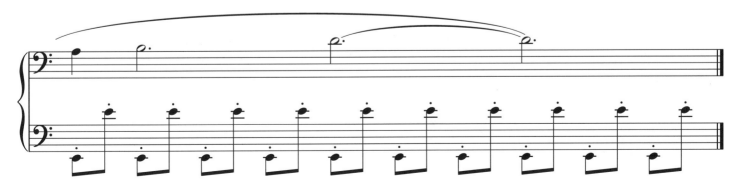

Sonata No.4 in A minor

A 'siciliana' is a dance from Sicily with a swaying rhythm, always in 6/8. Cimarosa wrote many keyboard sonatas. This one has several grace notes (*appoggiaturas*) which should always begin on the beat, with the left hand notes.

Domenico Cimarosa
(1749–1801)

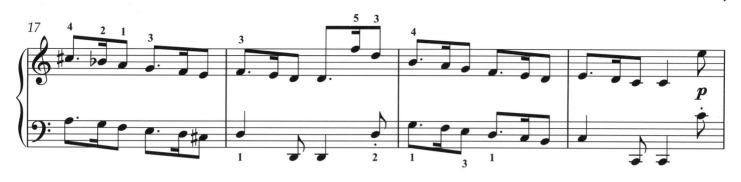

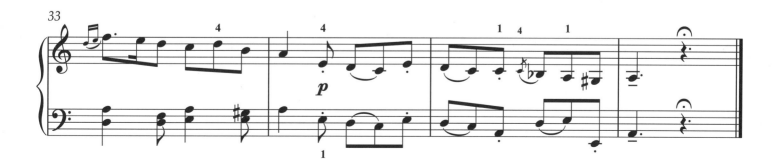

for Will Parsons

Steps

Put the sustain pedal down before you begin your journey. Your steps may sometimes be hesitant, and at other times more confident. No two bars of the piece are meant to sound the same rhythmically: make sure you play each one slightly differently, and try varying this from one performance to the next! Use the pauses to look ahead (perhaps to find a left-hand note that's coming up). Listen carefully to the overall sonority and enjoy the effect.

Julian Anderson
(b.1967)

con Ped. (hold down throughout the piece)

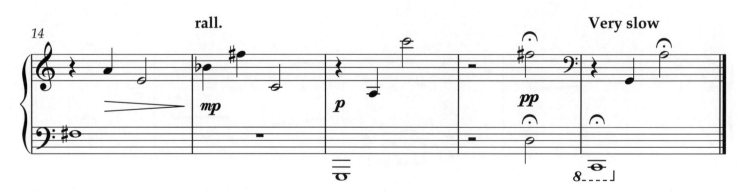

A joke
from **Mikrokosmos**

A lively and humorous piece, with three places where the music pauses for thought (each *poco rall.*).
Make up your own story for this piece – what do these bars/measures mean to you?

Béla Bartók
(1881–1945)

A trompet minuet

Clarke was the organist at St. Paul's Cathedral at the turn of the 18th century. The trumpet referred to in the title is probably a setting on the organ that imitates the sound of this brass instrument. Play short notes as a trumpeter would, and do not forget to breathe.

Jeremiah Clarke
(1674–1707)

The Italian bagpipers

'Towards Christmas, a group of strolling musicians come down from the mountains and play their bagpipes and oboes. They wear large, brown woollen coats and pointed hats.'

Charles Gounod
(1818–1893)

Norwegian couple
The husband

This pair of pieces presents the same music in two contrasted ways. The main difference is of course register – low for the husband and higher for the wife – but there are several others. How many can you spot?

Leo Ornstein
(1893–2002)

The wife

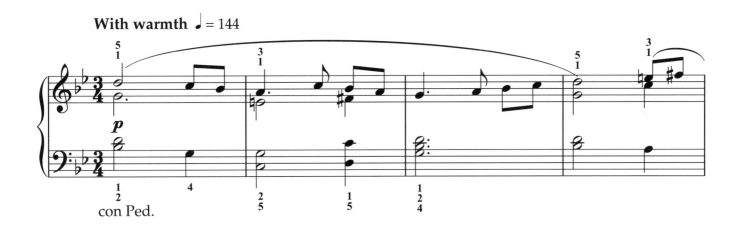

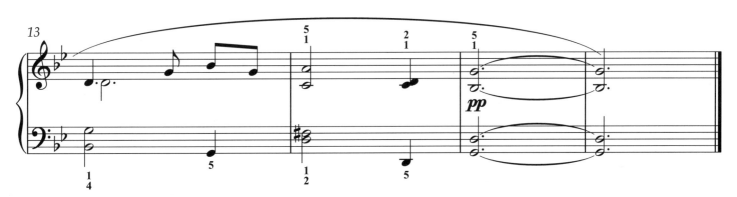

Hopscotch
from Fingerprints

When you play this jazzy little piece, imagine that your left hand is a plucked double bass. Make sure that the triplets in bars/measures 5 and 21 are really lazy and spaced out.

Richard Harris
(b.1968)

Prelude in E minor
BWV941, No.3

One of the many great things the piano can do is play more than one note at a time. Bach liked to write pieces with several independent lines running together. This piece has three (for a while in the middle, one of them takes a rest). Try to hear each one clearly as you play, remembering that each is as important as the other.

Johann Sebastian Bach
(1685–1750)

Minuet
from 20 Minuets D41, No.8

This is a minuet on a grand scale – imagine a full orchestral sound at the opening. Reserve your quietest singing sound for the trio (perhaps a solo flute?) and exaggerate the fortissimo when the full orchestra join in again. The effect should be funny – Schubert wrote lots of this kind of music as pure entertainment.

Franz Schubert
(1797–1828)

Trio

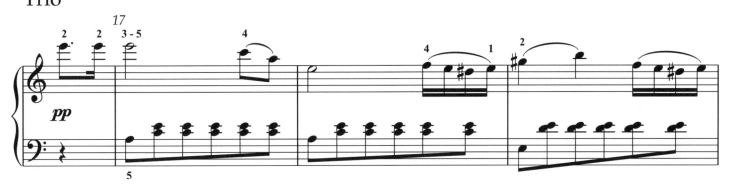

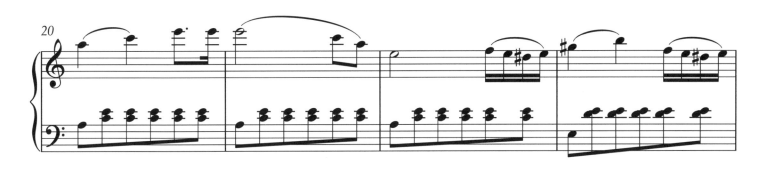

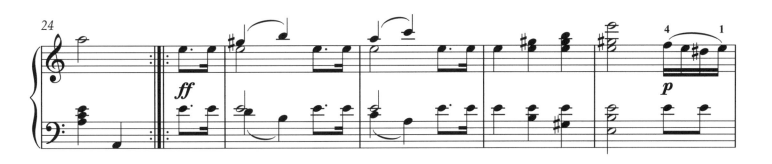

Menuetto D.C.

Transformations

Start by learning this series of chords, and practising changing the pedal smoothly. Once it feels familiar, have fun transforming the sequence into different styles of music. There are some suggested here, but do come up with some of your own.

John Lenehan
(b.1958)

* Play **f** like an organ (each chord con Ped.) or play **p** like a harp (arpeggiate each chord and play con Ped.)

The drummer

This piece, not surprisingly, is all about rhythm – but first you will need to find the notes in bars/measures 1–2, and 3–4. Then practise away from the piano by clapping on your knees or a table. The last chord can be played with a flat hand or your fist!

Jaroslava Luklova
(b.1936)

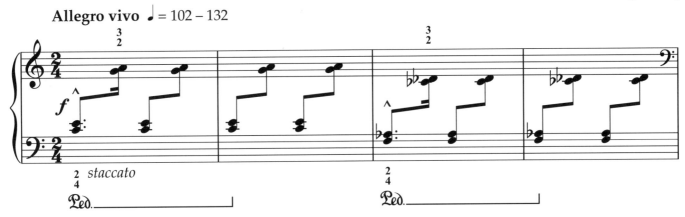

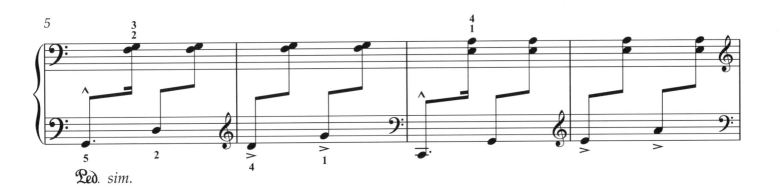

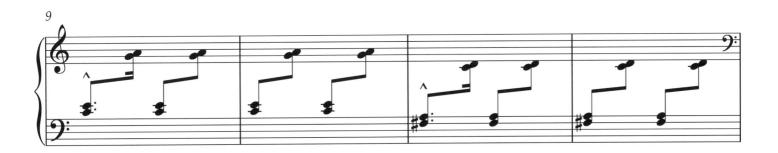

Gypsy dance

This boisterous dance is really effective if you exaggerate the dynamics. Notice how Haydn keeps changing from minor (bar/measure 1) to major (bar/measure 4). It is an energetic piece but does not need to go fast!

Joseph Haydn
(1732–1809)